Company

Company

Sam Ross

Sam R (signature)

for Rigg, with thanks (handwritten inscription)

Four Way Books
Tribeca

Library of Congress Cataloging-in-Publication Data

Names: Ross, Sam, 1985- author.
Title: Company / Sam Ross.
Description: New York, NY : Four Way Books, [2019]
Identifiers: LCCN 2018028726 | ISBN 9781945588334 (pbk. : alk. paper)
Classification: LCC PS3618.O84687 A6 2019 | DDC 811/.6--dc23
LC record available at https://lccn.loc.gov/2018028726

This book is manufactured in the United States of America and printed on acid-free paper.

Four Way Books is a not-for-profit literary press. We are grateful for the assistance
we receive from individual donors, public arts agencies, and private foundations.

Funding for this book was provided in part by a generous donation
in memory of John J. Wilson.

PROUD MEMBER

[clmp]

We are a proud member of the Community of Literary Magazines and Presses.

For my parents

Contents

III

IV

"Is the place that I have come to really Ithaca?"
—*The Odyssey*

"We drift in and out."
—Talking Heads

betrayed, it can kill
a man. In the Persian miniature,

Sol in Leo, the lion is its own
composite of animals

eaten by the lion: plaited
in the mane, woven in the tail,

folded inside haunches like
contortionists in an open-

walled box of hide. Uncover
enough of what you are

and the world won't think
to look for someone else.

REGARDING THE MURDER
OF YOUR BOYFRIEND'S ROOMMATE

He walked home at night and was circled
            by boys with knives who knifed him
                        and left him at someone's front door
in a neighborhood called Observatory,
            where he quickly bled to death.
                        From the observatory on the hill,
streets have what realtors call *expansive*
            grace, suburban streets of rosewood,
                        music. We would pour lighter fluid
in a circle around him every time
            he fell asleep on the beach with a beer
                        in his hand—but the circle never lit.
And though we meant it as a joke
            it wasn't a joke, it was devotion.
                        Had he survived, he would have been
a patient in Groote Schuur Hospital,
            site of the world's first heart transplant
                        in 1967. That patient died of complications
from pneumonia only eighteen
            days after his surgery, though they say
                        his new heart worked well till then.

Modern Medicine

Do not write permanent to describe the world
writes CA. Nothing is permanent.

I know that's right regarding apple, idol,
body language—

even the ones we wish would stay
when the scenery changes.

Whitman writes, if I had known them
I would have loved them.

Plenty gone to grass
but Andrew's alive—

he's eating fish sandwiches with me.
We laugh—shattered, glad, impermanent—

when I show him the scarlet
splashing harmless across my arms and chest.

RECOMMENDATION (NUMBER 9)

Some cities keep making musical chairs
of a home. Some money ends. Shortfall
and away we go. I belong

to a new house. The room lit by the red
roof of the house next door. The first night
three cards: *Magic, Lamentation,*

Liberty. Second night, I cut my hand
reaching for a knife above the shelf
hidden for the sake of a child.

Blood resists form, handful of mercury.
After the hurricane, I tried to
offer mine. After every

disaster, deferred—in spite of a red
sign that says *We are always in need.*

ADAPTATION, TEL AVIV

I squeeze the aloe
flesh over my knees

as your cousin scolds me
for saying *ocean*

when we are by a *sea*.
To me this is casual—

isn't it all the same water?—
to her it isn't.

What I could call her
is *colonist* since

it takes one to know.
Later, I wake when evening

still stains viridian
above the pink

and lemon neighborhood
to the *schhh*

of your grandfather's
slippers on tile which I hear

as the first soft syllable
of the name

we share. Six years
now you and I don't speak.

If I was not in love
there are secrets

a self keeps safe—
if I was you were right

to forget me.

SHIBBOLETH

In one life, I am engineer.
In one life, I am the only moving part.
If the soundtrack of the dream skips
out of sync or I am scared
sliding down interminably
everything can be altered lovingly
and the loving is called control.
But in my real life the skyline
is protean and too far past me.
Memory is the shadow greasing
his lip in a bar or the wet slur
when he read aloud. And if he spoke
of something strange, faces he saw
appearing out of wood grain
or other radiating lines I would stay
quiet, believing the blurred
forms of this world—shallow
depths of field, river-ruined colors—
can be crystallized only as long
as you keep moving. Who's to say
if it's enough? There is still
a risk when waking to melting
cells of frost that each
disappearance carries me closer

to forgetting completely
what was ours. A mind dilated
as the tips of peacock feathers,
and now with no voice left
on the telephone to tell me: *Yes,
that's how I remember it too.*

A Feast of Distance and Air

At the church of San Francisco
I lose my companion.
This morning on the red bed

I asked how to do anything
without doing damage.
I had a need

for ritual, wishing
to place blood and milk
in corners, bless keys

and feathers, choose
which cardinal direction
to face in sleep and sex.

In the parking lot
I get too lost in little videos.
A man directs cars.

See how devotion
enshrines even
the very recent past?

This one: dusked view
of the volcanic lake,
empty house embraced

by risen water, barking dog
on the porch—pacing—
the lights still on.

Water Street

I saw a python around a man
walking towards me

on Water Street
but it wasn't a snake

it was a ram's horn
the length of his arm

curling to his wrist.
Catching night-light, the horn

shone a silver scar across
gold-slicked ochre

and black. The man wore
a fine blue suit.

Because I had expected to see
one thing living

I was afraid
when it was another

made entirely of bone
that seemed to be crashing

in a field—a field
that was a part of the man

and also his covering,
a deep blue

battleground of silk and wool
where life touched life.

TRACE A LINE

Once, when I was home, my father told me: *You have the blood
of 100,000 innocent Iraqis on your hands.* This was confusing
because when I was twenty-one and flying into Harare,
he said that it would be *better* to join the army.
But I didn't, and I didn't understand the change of heart:
his slip between 'we're-all-in-this-together' and
'you're-here-on-your-own.' That evening I saw
a snake contorting itself around itself
over and over. Quickly, I warned my neighbor,
but she said she had already seen it. It had been
poisoned in her garage, and she had tossed it
over the fence into our yard. I wanted to ask
why she didn't lie when she had the chance,
it would have been easy enough, the right thing to do,
better than pretending the snake wasn't
a living thing dying in front of me, better than
admitting she had chosen our yard for that.
But I didn't ask her, I just nodded
and steered the mower in a wider perimeter
around the snake's seizing body.

Indiana, Not Indiana

Was it easier to ignore the sky stealing
      between hay bales? To mumble *heartland*
         heartland among the velvet kneecaps
of calves knocking up against your own,
      warm white bottle held in one hand
         a furred throat undulating greedily
in the other? In fact, it wasn't. Who would
      resist arrest in this sense: succumbing
         to the pleasure of astonishment. Then
in New York the squash flowers were
      soft orange lozenges stirred by taxis
         rustling headlights around First Ave's
isolated median. Indistinct conversation
      surrounded you, some rumor about a storm.
         Appetite pitched to a thrill for nightfall.

LIVESTREAM

Now, years from now, years ago, now again
we want to fathom breaking points.

We long to know what everyone wants
and how to get it. That's politics.

As my father says, *everyone's heart is larcenous.*
Today, they've decided something—

maybe it's not the same thing
but they've decided something. Material?

Unstoppable? Say anything:
I killed a man, I started a war, I disappeared

and now I'm back. Ask anything:
Who's next? What time in the morning?

And when we leave? Where will we go?
All afternoon I watch some run bravely

across the bridge. When the sun goes down
I turn on the projector, stay late

at the office with my friend
drinking wine, watching more. Maybe

it will come to *Nothing lasts forever.*
What do you remember?

As for tonight, people run against tanks
and the tanks turn back.

Time Expanding the Air Forcibly

I woke up in the white-hot middle of a summer
night. I saw the future fall apart.
Reality reasserted itself, a book's beginning.
In January, we ran to the Cloisters where
elevated views make the city a bed sheet
spread out tight and clean, hospital corners,
the colors pale and amiable then sudden:
yellow on blue. I showed you a picture I took
that day using the camera that leaks light
in a way that makes me want to cry,
makes me want to move to Mt. Fuji and paint
my life onto 8x10 transparencies.
About the picture, you said *that's how it felt,
but not how it looked.* How could that be?
I held the cold aperture-ring with my fingers
and pressed the shutter gently enough,
trusting to the chemicals on cold film
and the tenets of sympathetic magic.
I heard the *lock, click,* and *whisper.* I knew.
Later, the bartender asked us what we liked
and mapped our afternoon from there with
drinks with names like *Salt & Ash, the Heights,
The Horizon Was Like a Train on Fire.*

II

PILOT AND HYPNAGOGIA

In fact, science does not
distinguish between falling asleep
and waking. Scientifically

they are one phenomenon, each
with the capacity to paralyze.
There's rigor mortis

and then the hypnic twitch,
a lyric of imminent collision.
If there's a difference it isn't

empirical. Imagine somewhere
in the aviators' graveyard—
a billion splinters of glass planes

or the shards of a broken jaw.
What would the mouth say
if it weren't wired shut?

I tripped one day and became
certain as a train making its way
under the riverbed. It was years

before the feeling abated,
when our engine made a sound
I'd never heard before.

Tableau Vivant

Seemingly endless, this pose,
          but what I want is not
only my unbroken line.
          What I want is you to see

what is backlit, behind me.
          Not the silhouette—
but the negative space
          I make blocking light.

A glimpse of the thin
          boundary between witness
and essence. You can see
          what I love by the way

I decide what is worth
          living for. This is not
a trick—I can sense how far
          we are from the end.

What I want is you to see
          the flame tucking
itself in. What I want is you
          to see the fuse alight

and in reverse. Before you
        a burning pinwheel
reels back to its beginning.
        Look at me.

After Assault

Less the blood than the timing.

Running till my mouth unlatched in the street.

Each exhalation in the cold became
a charmed shape. Leafless linden in air.

Winter interest landscape architects call
the spectacle of bare trees

—in childhood the legs of the stillborn foals
branching out of the wheelbarrow.

Overturned, a bucket freed bottle flies

feasting on the afterbirth. Quick to flee—

dark swarm on a path no one else could see.

STRUCK

Sometimes, still, I hold my hand to my eyes
so the sun becomes another thing sewn up
tied inside. I am making a mystery
where none exists.

*

To see can only be piece-by-piece.
To see an icepick shine, shine, shine.
Recognition is sly, mimicking the edge
between a door & jamb

holding back the empty hall
as if to say *don't come any closer*—
but they did.

*

I held fast to what was safe
when I was safe. I gave up the ghosts
that should have remained reminders
of the randomness in each piece
of the world.

& blood wheeled around my iris.
& a blood-spoiled oasis
became the bargain struck by day
dimming days into another year.

*

Then: cell by cell the scar allays
its ridge of pink to white.

*

Then: I know what kind of world it is
by the sound of its emergencies:
Doppler waves of sirens,
red breaking blue.
The box fan bends the smoke
from oil drum barbecues
into anchors that strike the bottom
of my lungs.

*

What it means to change?
I wanted to kill
the air for touching me
until I couldn't
remember differently

& now what remains
is the comedy of it.

How blood filled my eyes
the morning after the night
I said *love*
the very first time.

Lichtung

Here the message is written on trees. Somewhere else
is where the tide can overtake you. There is where

I drowned and drowned.

                    There is where catastrophe

amalgamates in the dark, and here is thereafter.
I waited so long to re-measure the cold current

tunneling its obsession, clear of weather. I would say it
like this: *the waves were larger for their namelessness,*

but you said it best, Alexander, here,

                       where you said

you can't always get what you haunt. Here is where I am
different, done, and undoing. A stock of bone and root

sifted in muslin, sheer

               as the cone of air tipping a rocket

rising through ozone, vivified, like blood passing
long halls of marrow at night,

                              not knowing where.

Still Animals

In the chicken coop, Jill and I found a headless one.
We cleaned up, and she told me it's what skunks do—

snap a neck in their jaws, twist the head off.
They guzzle the yellow fluid from the eggs. They leave

the carcass untouched but lap up the blood
as if it was honey. How could I pretend it wasn't a thrill

to hear this in the morning? It came back to me after
I received your letter, the one cataloguing shapes

our bodies make together at night. I imagined
red threads tied to each of a bird's talons, then to us

arranged in the position you called your favorite:
my mouth at your neck, barely, and you feigning sleep.

Common Law

Elizabeth laughs at the news:
how it has made everyone so happy,
the pre-school in a nursing home.

As though people were meant to live together!
As though we needed each other. At my office
we debate flesh: if flesh

is muscle, or animal, or else
any material that shapes the living
or living-ish—flesh of seeds,

flesh of washed fruit. Bird flesh,
turtle flesh, fire flesh. The train
fresh with the smell of cucumbers

crunched out of a paper bag
by father and daughter—
it all makes me think of someone

whose house I ran past until
flesh became our common world.
These days I keep three crystal bowls

lined on the windowsill.
Absent flesh, I kiss their prisms, I kiss
the comets they cast to the floor.

ARTERIAL

Did the dogs' feet blister?
Small stain, mottle of blood—
a cardinal seen from far away?
No, they lap the field
uninjured, reveling in some other
mark of quarry. Red began
Percival's history of astonishment—
a color that can arrest,
empty and break an armor.
Most everything else is
drained, water-damaged, white
except this light flashing
on the plane of snow.
It was goose blood
that blushed the field
and fixed the knight to it.
An arrow led him
to red reflections, reflections
left him there.

Mercy Error

Caught on a long oak branch, fishing line in a freak-knot
around the heron's foot

snared the bird. We hope it thrashed to death quickly—

better than starving.

By one leg it must have dangled for weeks. No one
at home to save it or see:

        slack wings spinning,
a wall of red creeper,

        feathers descending gray September.
Lacking a rifle, we delay shooting the line

to bring the slaughtered thing down.

        The gun comes from our neighbor's house.

EXCHANGE

Gaps in delphinium along a ridge

        dim the difference between blue flowers

and little apertures to the sea.

        I almost wrote ocean. One day, a man

considered desertion, the next

        he deserted. In return for his release,

five others cross the ocean. I almost

        wrote sea. When planes pass in the sky

or meet in disaster, these are details

        you can't discern from kissing.

BLACK'S BEACH

Stripped to swim in the cindered morning,
     we go slack in whitecaps.

     Then swept far from our clothes,
we lose them. *Who-will-help-us-and-how*

     comes after *have-we-lost-the-plot.*
     No more wanting what we thought.

We hike up a switchback naked.
     Bluffs break past silver rows of fog

     burning between cars. It is no dream
we know, the sea—never still or safe

     or finished with us. Just this once—
     seconds merely—when the breakers mute:

the sky is clear, the water is clear.

Bowers v. Hardwick

I've learned cause and effect.
I know because the parade-float
is outside my window, brass snorkels
catch the light of the sky like a bell.

There will be pieces of pink paper
in the street, and some will melt
after the day's rain and some will burn
on into the night. How could it be otherwise?

I know we endured all the words—
and we must forget them for now,
as if they were skywriting, fading white.

Some urge us, some warn us not to transgress
what is deeply unspeakable.
But then, who am I going to talk to here?

Someone turn on the radio, someone
sing with me—please.

Or we can just spend a day
drawing dirty pictures of each other.
There's time. Wasn't it you
who promised me the music would last
all afternoon?

SHIVER, SHELTER

My ghost refuses
to fall in love with statues

anymore, or anyone.
He claims

we are the same as we were
in the 90s, says,

Your father
moves decisively as I pass through

ten thousand walls.
Solar warmth surrounds

my fingers with rings.
Everyone looks

at the blue linen
hanging on my back.

I pass. I have not forgotten how
to trick even myself,

like a peony opening
on the landing

because it lacks an instrument
to sense the paleness,

or sense to know better.
How do you stay decent and still

refuse everyone all
of the time?

Vox Celestis

I have tried to do no harm
but sparks fall from an overpass

under night construction
into the light of cars. It goes on—

for now, for good, forever—
but in this heat what wouldn't I steal

for ten seconds of kissing? Once
I drove through an Arizona

made blue by unusual rain.
It was after cruelty

when a stranger said to me:
I'm just one in a world filled with this.

III

CURRICULUM

Of course it's fucked, the past.
Years nagging the back of your neck—

they come, how they come . . .
After Hector was slain

he was said to be softer
than when he burned ships—

I'm not talking about ships.
I'm talking about ash in the shape of a man.

Or the next dream:
clouds coiling through a mountain pass

revealing the landscape's real form—
indifference. The rains today:

remarkable not for the rains
but for the wind that turned up the ground

making signs of what was disregarded:
receipts, results, petals and powders

strung like streamers hooked on the air.
I would learn *rare*

and *love* and *want* and *wait*.
I had to start at the beginning.

CAPTIVE PATTERN

Probably many someones forgave
my hometown king of used cars

his seasonal commercials.
His chained tiger grown seven years

older every summer.
I never did. And the others—

just this forgetting.
Have a Good Life, Baby.

*

I'm losing the game I play
that begins before dark.

How far can I run counting scrub oaks
to prime numbers

before roadside forests net lights
the way tigers are netted,

before I can't see
the road leading home.

*

Nightfall was always what came
from saying *nightfall*.

ENUCLEATION

In a shop near a church
        in the center of a city

I blinded myself.

        I held a penlight
against my left eye.

        I always craved the red

drape I could make
        shining lamps through skin.

I pressed its switch—

        click—it unzipped
a spring-loaded blade from within

        its heart. Haven't you ever

reached for light and reached
        an end instead,

a bright bayonet?

POLAROID (BONDAGE, C. 1973)

Enough like recognition—
wolf-white eye smear

        two stops overexposed.
        He thinks he is quicker

than the flash,
thinks he was more than crumpled

        blue cotton by the glass door—
        ghost-color of dried semen

the end of the afternoon
in March. More than

        the total fractal of his folded
        nakedness—

muscle on drywall,
a tightening of knots.

        Is something slowly named
        in his mouth or has he

forgotten? Forgotten,
he is past holding

        the posture of someone
        who changes appreciably,

someone named at his stages
like a star.

Company

If it wanted a companion what the whale got
was us regarding its beam of bone:

ten feet blotched with hide,
capped pink with seal-gnawed meat,

washed up at Pilgrim Heights. Though the bone
would not generate. Would not

be lit by the moon's white cords
and accumulate flesh, weight,

more bones. Would not be rolled in
a carpet of salt and dragged seaward

to allay an ache so great it gave grounds
for sacrifice. Because the animal was dead.

The rib, what we saw of it. Apart
from the *flesh of my flesh* bit

in Genesis, the only book
the word *rib* appears in the King James

is Daniel's: the king's dream
of tempest-wrecked seas

out of which emerged horrible beasts—
one, a bear holding ribs in its teeth—

a vision that troubled Daniel
though he kept his distress to himself—

which I cannot when—
under a photo of you looking down at the bone—

I write on my phone and then a bear appears
in place of the word *Ours*.

THE OPPOSITE OF BLEEDING

When he wanted to talk he put on his shirt
and he walked up the road

to see the stones' brief lifelines
etched below rudimentary angels.

Another quarter mile and the jetty
blistered with shells, glossy hearts thumbed

half purple, half the white of bone.
Placing one shard across another,

he covered their creamy parts
so only a dark center shone:

violet eye, violet star.
He called the star Bruiser.

He called the star Scorcher.
He called the star Time to Eat and Live.

And the sharp grasses of a salt-crushed marsh,
the saline swell risen to the waterline

of his wind-reddened eyes—
they were like the rain begun long before

he felt it seeping through his clothes
to his hair and his skin.

STORYTELLING

This year, your father the age
of his father when—

     he says, *On Thursday I'll be sixty-seven.*

You're on the shore; he's on an inland river.
He bought a skiff he rows.

     You run the shore.

Movement makes a mind biddable.
Landlocked less. The year starts in October.

     You want to ask: *but how did he do it?*

What year? Where were the brothers
who were his sons? A sea unscaled,

     no suicide story, one thousand miles

inland to the river. In the skiff
he rows without shoes. *So one day your father—?*

     No answer. You run the shore,

leap back too late to evade white foam;
new shoes, soaked.

On the river, he grips the oars.

His name was his name
then his name was yours.

PRO TEM

I was the paperback next to your figurines.
One dozen cassettes packed in a shoebox.
I could pack up quickly.

I was your tenant, your boarder.
Convenient, your roomer.
A good sleeper-in.

Could sharpen the rusted instruments.
Knitting needles, a proper cheese knife.
To me, the lawns always looked to be waiting
        for blankets or rain.

What home I made myself.
What for.
When I was grounds-walker, garden-watcher.

Your disciple of eaves, occupant
        taking air in near the tent and colored lights.
Bandleader, hornblower,

the whole of an invited and thirsty crowd.
I was groom, bride, oath-taker, years-
        past prime. Deposit. Fondness. A check.

I was your guest.

Accompanied

Past the ten thousand days? Yes.
Still, it comes—passes—

comes—*thrill*—
like seven great humpbacks

hoisting above the surface
their corroded spades.

How did it come to this?
The boat fumes' near-

erotic choke, opal shine
of the wandered-out tide?

Anyone waiting
in a base-gathered

glimmer-pool grows
more mirage than reflection

more approximate
than indigo—

so—see—
how alone can you be?

NOVEMBERED

The boy wore his costume of "Are You the Boy?" in eyeliner
over his forehead. The bar didn't blink.

Living things escaped no thanks to his ache for them.
Some became far-flung; others, still swam.

Pitter-patter in the dark: wind pinching the house
or rats scratching in from the wind.

The poems had been longer and illumined.
Was that gluttony in their pockets? *are you exhausted to see me?*

The longer he listened the better he heard voices he could do nothing with.
To be parted from the thing, remained inside.

How roving the road's contour. How bedlam the migrations.
Nights, he rehearsed escape. Passwords for the letter-lock cuffs:

Payback. Flinch. Feast.
What he did when the animals came in,

what he didn't know, what was impossible to forget.
Chime, shine, then bolt: a sheaf of swords fired down his throat.

ATTENDANT

We were in bed with the baby, the lights low, both of us holding one of
  her rabbit feet.

Give them free and fair or something close and revenge is what they'll take.
  Their turn.

In the morning I drove back north to my green pearl room.

You took a wrong turn to get here, a woman at the station said.

I froze and she nodded at the license plate on my truck. *How do you like it*
  here?

At the pump I fudged the credit card, then gave the code to the cashier.

And the last four digits, she said. *And a fingerprint,* she laughed. *And your*
  blood, she laughed.

A Taste

Weren't the mussels rich enough?
How about the carbonara?

The tomatoes, the butter tart,
osso bucco—that shank?

I dragged my teeth on bone,
cut my tongue for iron, marrow.

Savored … but no, it wasn't enough.
So I held his shoulders down,

that weight. He had
a good half-foot on me

and knelt. I don't say tender—
that's for meat—

but there was readiness,
an eager gratitude.

I'm not the only one
who's seen both sides of *feed*:

68

take or *give*. I left the door
unlocked and gave.

Fed him to feed,
a neighborhood stray.

LAST CALL

I'll stay too long before leaving.
I took a little something.

Jaw still clenched
two weeks since

teeth last ground in ecstasy.
The feeling like when

there was money
then less of it, then less.

The bar awaiting another
thumbprint drawn across

gin-slicked mahogany.
Clientele awaiting

moonlight, dimming.
Should surfacing last

as long as this? Say nothing—
nothing—nothing to fear

is no reason to stay—
but I won't be giving my ticket away.

It means I'm good
for another.

IV

Vox Erotica

Did I fill my mouth with salt?
Did I equate night and affinity?

Were there two lampposts in the forest?
Did I need to be right

or did I dare abandon? What bewilders
a compass? What good is

a life spent tracing the light
on friends' faces fading in the street?

When a lover asks you
to wash your feet before bed

will you sleep? Imagine clotheslines?
Weren't the lakes north of here

named after legends
who had drowned in them?

Sext

I believe this
to be real as anything
but safe. It's like
Puccini: we're so close
to the moon up here
let me tell you who
I am—and guess
about you: do you like
to fable—I mean
danke—I mean
dance? What I like
is not knowing
what we look like
to each other. Isn't it
that way anyway?
I saw silverberries
so high atop stones
they were black
against the sky.
Limbs, finger-thin.
More evidence
never hurt a case
for handsome but
by the time you

reach me, I may be
somewhere else.
You might not even
know—like sleeping
in a tent on a dune
moving miles through
the night. Or now
when I'm close. Are you
close?

OPTIMISM

She said she sensed she was
      breathing easy
      walking the horse &
I thought she meant
      she was ashamed
      savoring a moment
of pleasure during crisis—
      wandering under
      animal-shadow, cool
at the road's shoulder
      since what their tie offered
      was the opposite
of tenuous—brass-
      capped braid clicked
      to harness, hanging slack
like wrecked wire
      strung from the heavy
      circle of his jaw
to her grip allowed
      by his nature—kind—
      to be light—but she
had meant *schadenfreude,*
      laugh riot—her vision
      of the new fool—no one

should *be* President—reduced

    to retreat-and-skulk,

      his palace, stupid, beaten.

Couldn't it be fun

    a little, watching ruin?

      I envied her then—

I envied her again.

Winter Scene

So cold today
our warm century
takes imagining.

Closer to truth
here underground
where the manager

of the banya
pulls down
the towel over

a bare blue bulb—
cornflower glow
unmuted, haloed now

with steam.
He calls men animals.
One animal digs

his nail in a tangerine
another carves
in scum a code

or scrawl
something like
a promise of language

that carries my eye
up the white walls
to imagine the silver

roof open to snow
storm or skyline
then down

the courses and bonds
of outer brickwork.
Room or cell. A cold century.

It needs no imagining.
Some men in their beds,
some men in their prison beds.

A Preference

His sperm pooled alive and shining

like milk glass in a ridge of
his abdomen.

We spoke quietly.

Such a sour thing to hear
in the afterglow

of personal kissing—

after I'd come
to love the afternoon stranger—

how my skin looked
to him in the light

how clean—

did he really mean it—
how perfectly

white.

EQUESTRIAN

He's beautiful—
but his legs are wrong, says my mother

when I show her a picture
of what my friend the sculptor made

out of chicken wire and plaster, a life-size horse.
In a pickup, my friend and I circled the marsh,

beast in the bed she rode
red-jumpsuit-and-velvet-helmeted

as if she was a fox chaser.
She didn't mean to look so fascist.

What made the horse wrong
was the angle of his knees

or something off with the fetlocks
or other slight accommodations made to support

the weight of the medium.
That horses walk at all is a wonder.

That we ride them, another. If he was real—
You'd have to shoot him, says my mother.

National Geographic

I am in the clinic
in a slate gray room

reading a magazine story
about young Russians.

There is a picture
of a Moscow couple

dressed in fox costumes
for erotic play. They wear clothes

but their heads are covered
in orange and white fur helmets

with blue and gold glassy eyes,
their black noses glossed

to mimic animal shine—
is there a word

for a mask like that?
Around the whole head? A helmet

but also a disguise?
Their hands and feet

are covered, too, in paws.
I think of the poem

Elizabeth Bishop wrote
about being a little girl

in a waiting room
reading a *National Geographic*

and photos of volcanoes
and breasts make her realize

something frightening
about her name and the future

of her body. It's winter
in Massachusetts in that poem.

It's winter in Massachusetts here.
I can't tell, really,

if those foxes are like New York
where you can find anything

if you go looking or if
animal-dressing really is

a sex craze sweeping
coupled, young, straight Russians.

"The War was on," the poem's end
begins and one can end

any poem like that and still
tell the truth.

A woman comes to me
and wraps a blue band

around my bicep, two-finger kneads
my arm to prime a vein

and slides her butterfly needle
above the crook of my elbow,

drawing enough garnet-
colored fluid to fill two tubes

and I remember someone
begging me to come

inside—*Please, please, come in*—
when all I thought was *Shut up,*

why won't you just please shut up
and I am ashamed

of an angry thought like that
though I don't think

I could have felt differently,
not then, and now at the clinic

it is dark with storm
near four outside and still

a war is on.

Vox Inaudita

From jet lag, from all-sky,
my mind is baled

and back to this: I'm filled with awe.
Time-travel is following

glow-tape trails down the stairwell—
a fingernail moving flush

along a ribbon or tendon—
but I can't feel my own beating heart

even with both hands on it.
Hanging off the high dive

I re-encounter each assembling whisper.
When the moon sinks below sea level

I know the veiled code—
how to hijack the jukebox to repeat,

repeat. Teach me to forget
I'm lost here.

INNAMORATO

We are three
>   on the cape's east side at sunset.

Valley of pink shadow.
>   Zuhair finds tree roots &

lifts them up,
>   a crown of antlers he drops

like a shedding buck.

>   We leave
when we no longer

>   have faces.

Sea cliffs raise a black screen.
>   The sky exposes

its assortment
>   of keys.

*

We were three

      in June in Brighton
on a blanket, not saying a word

      in the sun. In ultraviolet.
Inviolate.

The waves curled,
      kept leaving. No song

on the radio. World

      slayed smaller
Orlando

      Orlando

Vox Fidelis

What god I loved I loved only for a time.

                                  Suppose again.

Suppose at the end of all this were lamps. A gold room
winter readied between trains and the road.

And if we were obliged to abide by decisions made in our dreams—
what then?

                                      trouble when the sun sinks?
trouble made snow-bright? trouble in a Brooklyn bigger than our minds?

Faith was never easy—so I never had any

                                    but I can see rupture seam to scar
                                    and call it plenty.

If snowdrifts build by morning I'll begin a new flirtation
with the ordinary world.

SWIMMING

Now that the bay is blue again
you feel less like a shadow
making any boot heel home—

and there's the moon
even at noontime!
Little house at the edge of the wharf

postered with portraits
of fisherman's wives. You like her best,
the only wife smiling.

Rusted-orange chains connect
concrete and water
where you walk balance-beaming

above the ultramarine.
To the one who touches your arms
you could even say, before diving in,

I'm think I'm getting stronger.

ONLY THE PAST CAN SAVE YOUR LIFE

Call history this:

      insistence regarding desire

      not to be forgotten.

Morning in the Village

      imagining those I never knew—

      all we have forgotten.

Rooms won't stay emptied.

      Honey spills through iron to photos—

      twenty years, thirty.

Rosemary and sugar

      taste the same.

      Salt falls on cherry.

Rooms asked how

      could I continue

      what had been interrupted

and I answered, a *Tempest's* Miranda, a fool to weep

      at what makes me glad—

      and *glad*—though I began

to call something like the past mine
      only recently. Little history—
      sweep it from the floor—

put the light in me.

Notes

"Modern Medicine" references CAConrad's essay in verse "Poetry and Ritual."

"Recommendation (Number 9)": from the Food and Drug Administration's *Revised Recommendations for Reducing the Risk of Human Immunodeficiency Virus Transmission by Blood and Blood Products* which prohibits men who have sex with men from making blood donations.

"Time Expanding the Air Forcibly" takes its title from the song "Half Asleep" by School of Seven Bells.

"Lichtung" takes its title from a German word meaning a clearing or glade.

"Exchange": In 2014, an American soldier held captive since 2009 was traded for five Guantanamo detainees.

"Bowers v. Hardwick": the 1986 Supreme Court case that upheld a Georgia law criminalizing sodomy. Lawrence v. Texas overturned the decision in 2003.

"Curriculum": From Book XXII of *The Iliad*, as the Achaeans gaze upon and mutilate the corpse of Hector, translated by Alston H. Chase and William G. Perry, Jr.: "And thus one would speak, glancing at his neighbor: 'Hector is much softer to touch than when he burned the ships with blazing fire.' So one would say, and deal him a wound as he stood beside him."

"Polaroid (Bondage c. 1973)": Robert Mapplethorpe's.

"Company": Daniel's vision of the four beasts, King James Version: "And behold another beast, a second, like to a bear, and it raised up itself on one side, and it had three ribs in the mouth of it between the teeth of it: and they said thus unto it, Arise, devour much flesh."

"Winter Scene": Martin Wong's.

"Equestrian" references the video "Who Tows the Wagon?" by Becky Sellinger.

Acknowledgments

Thank you to the editors of the publications in which some of the poems in this book first appeared:

Bat City Review, Beloit Poetry Journal, Boston Review, FIELD, Denver Quarterly, Grist, Gulf Coast, Guernica, Hunger Mountain, Lambda Literary, New Republic, Paperbag, Southern Humanities Review, The Volta, The Offing, Tin House, Tuesday; An Art Project, Vinyl, Visible Binary, Washington Square Review, and *Waxwing.*

To those who gave encouragement, insight, company, and love during the long making. They include but are not limited to those listed here. For leading by example, all my admiration and affection:

Patrick Abatiell, Kirkwood Adams, Jerriod Avant, Ari Banias, E.C. Belli, Marina Blitshteyn, William Brewer, Jamel Brinkley, MRB Chelko, Iris Cushing, Timothy Donnelly, Hilary Dobel, Sasha Fletcher, Jay Deshpande, Carolina Ebeid, Josh and Nalini Edwin, Kelly Forsythe, Jenny George, Hafizah Geter, Julia Guez, CoryAnne Harrigan, John Fenlon Hogan, Alice Sola Kim, Akil Kumarasamy, Catherine Lacey, Ricardo Maldonado, Philip Matthews, Rosalie Moffett, Brian Mooney, Matt Morton, Morgan Parker, Jennifer Pan, Tommy Pico, Jacques Rancourt, Camille Rankine, Montana Ray, Ellis Rosen, Austen Rosenfeld, Margaret Ross, Andrew Russell, Megan Savage, Becky Sellinger, Solmaz Sharif, Jayson Smith, Noah Stetzer, Ryann Stevenson, Phillip B. Williams, Lauren Wilkinson, Elizabeth Clark and Märten Wessel.

To the team at Four Way Books for their diligence and care and to Patrick Leger for the cover.

To my many teachers—including Richard Howard, Cate Marvin, and Ellen Bryant Voigt—for their own poems and for pushing me onward, and to Carl Phillips for hearing something here.

To my friends at the Academy of American Poets, Asian American Writers' Workshop, *Blunderbuss Magazine, Circumference: Poetry in Translation,* the

Bread Loaf Writers' Conference, Indiana University, Columbia University School of the Arts, and the Fine Arts Work Center in Provincetown.

To my friends who are my family and to my family, for giving me everything.

And to Lucie Brock-Broido, for opening the door. I remain your Samuel.

Sam Ross has received fellowships and support from Columbia University, the Bread Loaf Writers' Conference, the Watermill Center, and the Fine Arts Work Center in Provincetown. His work has appeared in the *New Republic, Denver Quarterly, Tin House*, and elsewhere. He grew up in Indiana and lives in New York City.

Publication of this book was made possible by grants and donations. We are also grateful to those individuals who participated in our 2018 Build a Book Program. They are:

Anonymous (11), Sally Ball, Vincent Bell, Jan Bender-Zanoni, Kristina Bicher, Laurel Blossom, Adam Bohanon, Betsy Bonner, Mary Brancaccio, Lee Briccetti, Jane Martha Brox, Carla & Steven Carlson, Caroline Carlson, Stephanie Chang, Tina Chang, Liza Charlesworth, Andrea Cohen, Machi Davis, Marjorie Deninger, Patrick Donnelly, Charles Douthat, Emily Flitter, Lukas Fauset, Monica Ferrell, Jennifer Franklin, Helen Fremont & Donna Thagard, Robert Fuentes & Martha Webster, Ryan George, Panio Gianopoulos, Chuck Gillett, Lauri Grossman, Julia Guez, Naomi Guttman & Jonathan Mead, Steven Haas, Lori Hauser, Mary & John Heilner, Ricardo Hernandez, Deming Holleran, Nathaniel Hutner, Janet Jackson, Rebecca Kaiser Gibson, David Lee, Jen Levitt, Howard Levy, Owen Lewis, Sara London & Dean Albarelli, David Long, Katie Longofono, Cynthia Lowen, Ralph & Mary Ann Lowen, Jacquelyn Malone, Fred Marchant, Donna Masini, Catherine McArthur, Nathan McClain, Richard McCormick, Victoria McCoy, Britt Melewski, Kamilah Moon, Beth Morris, Rebecca Okrent, Gregory Pardlo, Veronica Patterson, Jill Pearlman, Marcia & Chris Pelletiere, Maya Pindyck, Megan Pinto, Taylor Pitts, Eileen Pollack, Barbara Preminger, Kevin Prufer, Vinode Ramgopal, Martha Rhodes, Peter & Jill Schireson, Jason Schneiderman, Jane Scovel, Andrew Seligsohn & Martina Anderson, Soraya Shalforoosh, James Snyder & Krista Fragos, Ann St. Claire, Alice St. Claire-Long, Dorothy Tapper Goldman, Robin Taylor, Marjorie & Lew Tesser, Boris Thomas, Judith Thurman, Susan Walton, Calvin Wei, Bill Wenthe, Allison Benis White, Elizabeth Whittlesey, Rachel Wolff, Hao Wu, Anton Yakovlev, and Leah Zander.